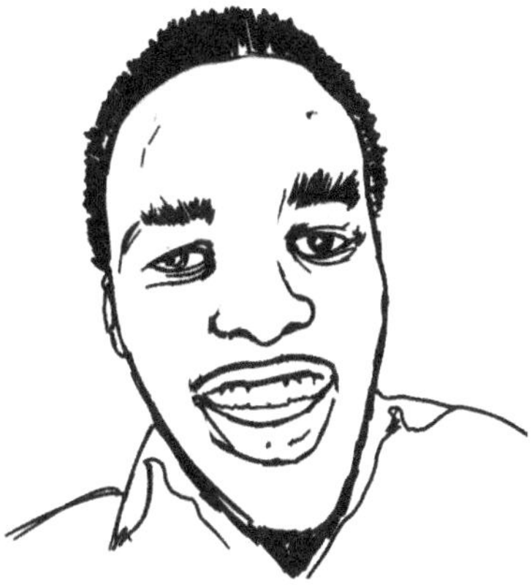

Hi there, my name is Jeff.
I hope you enjoy this coloring book.

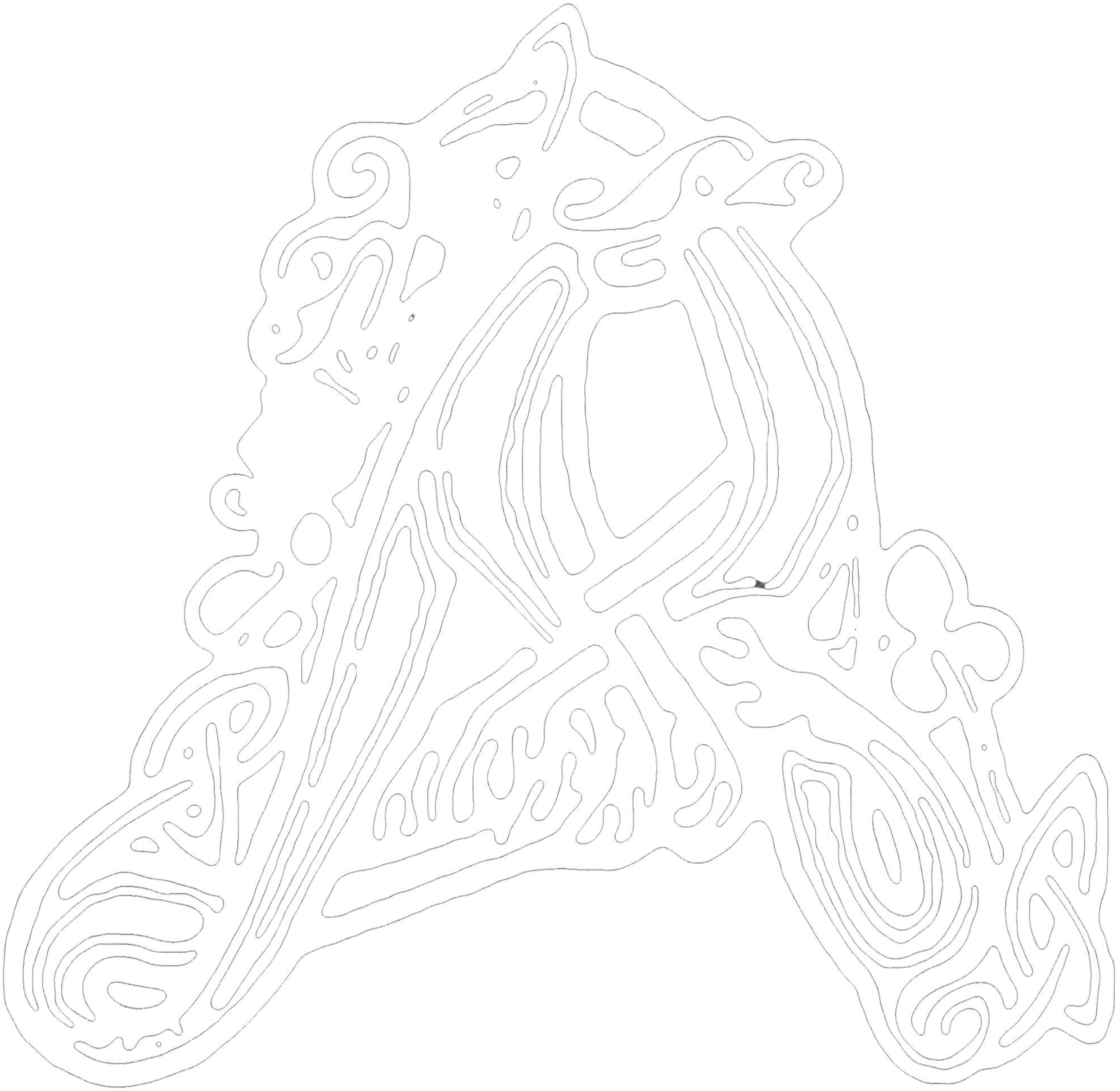

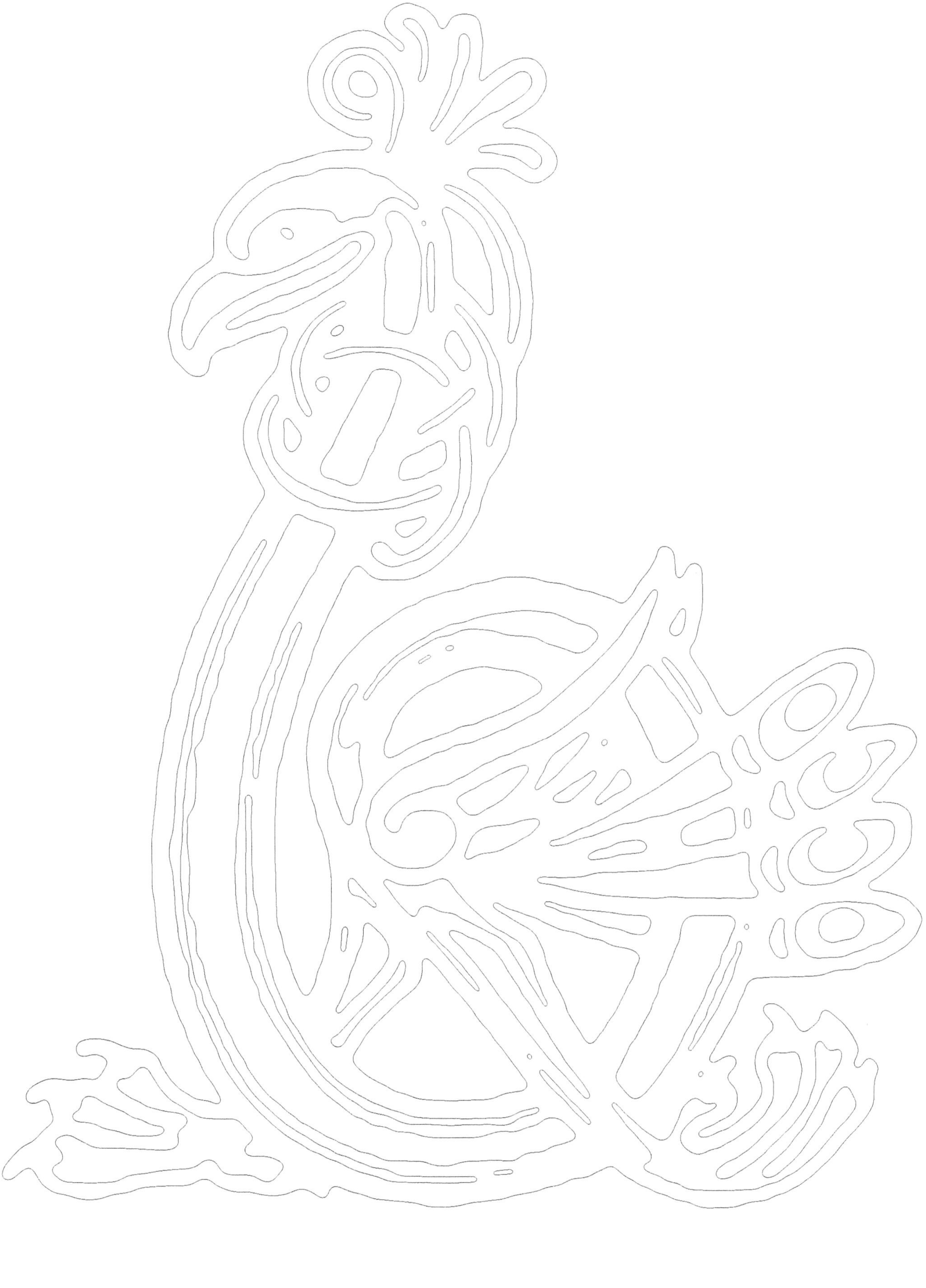

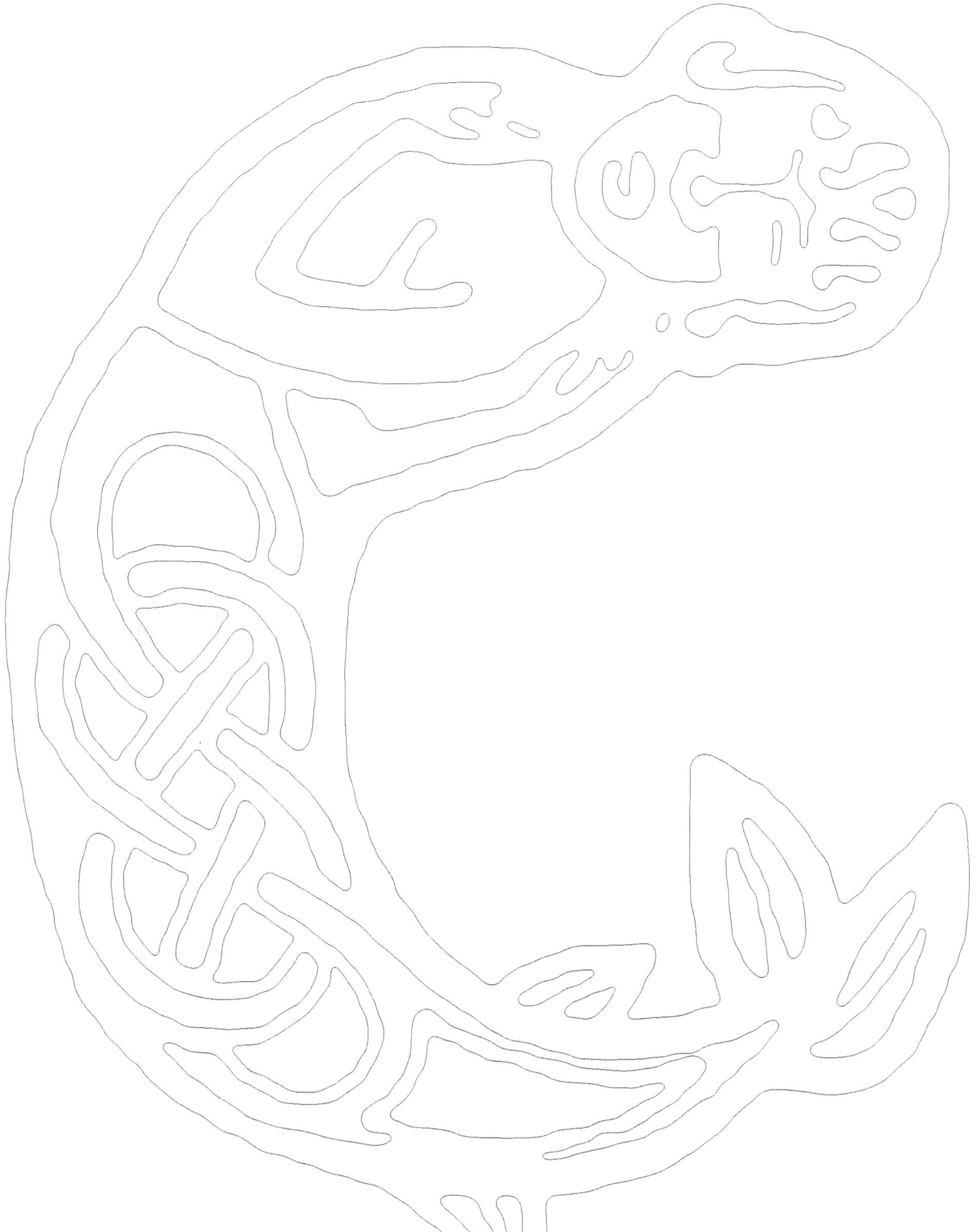

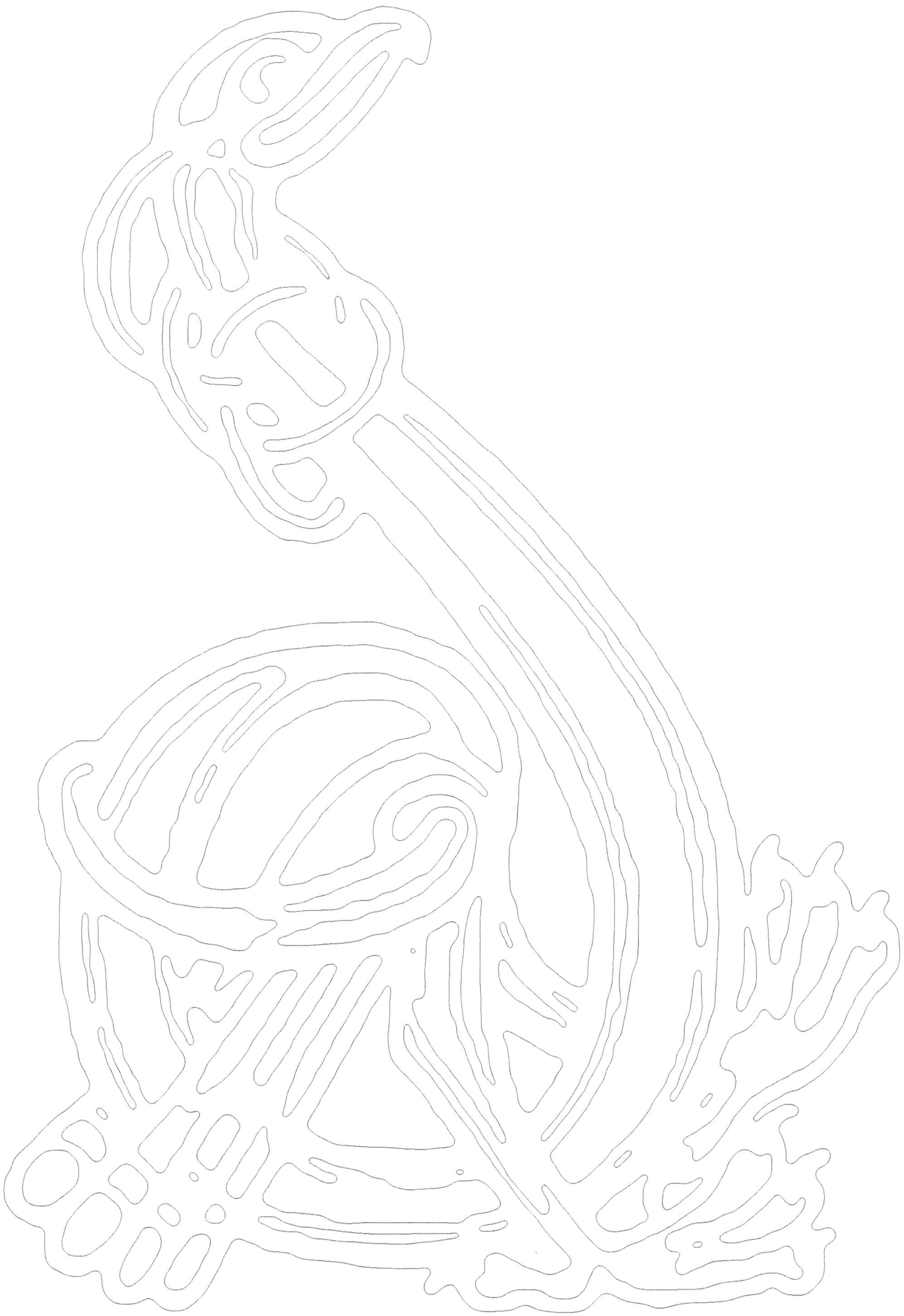

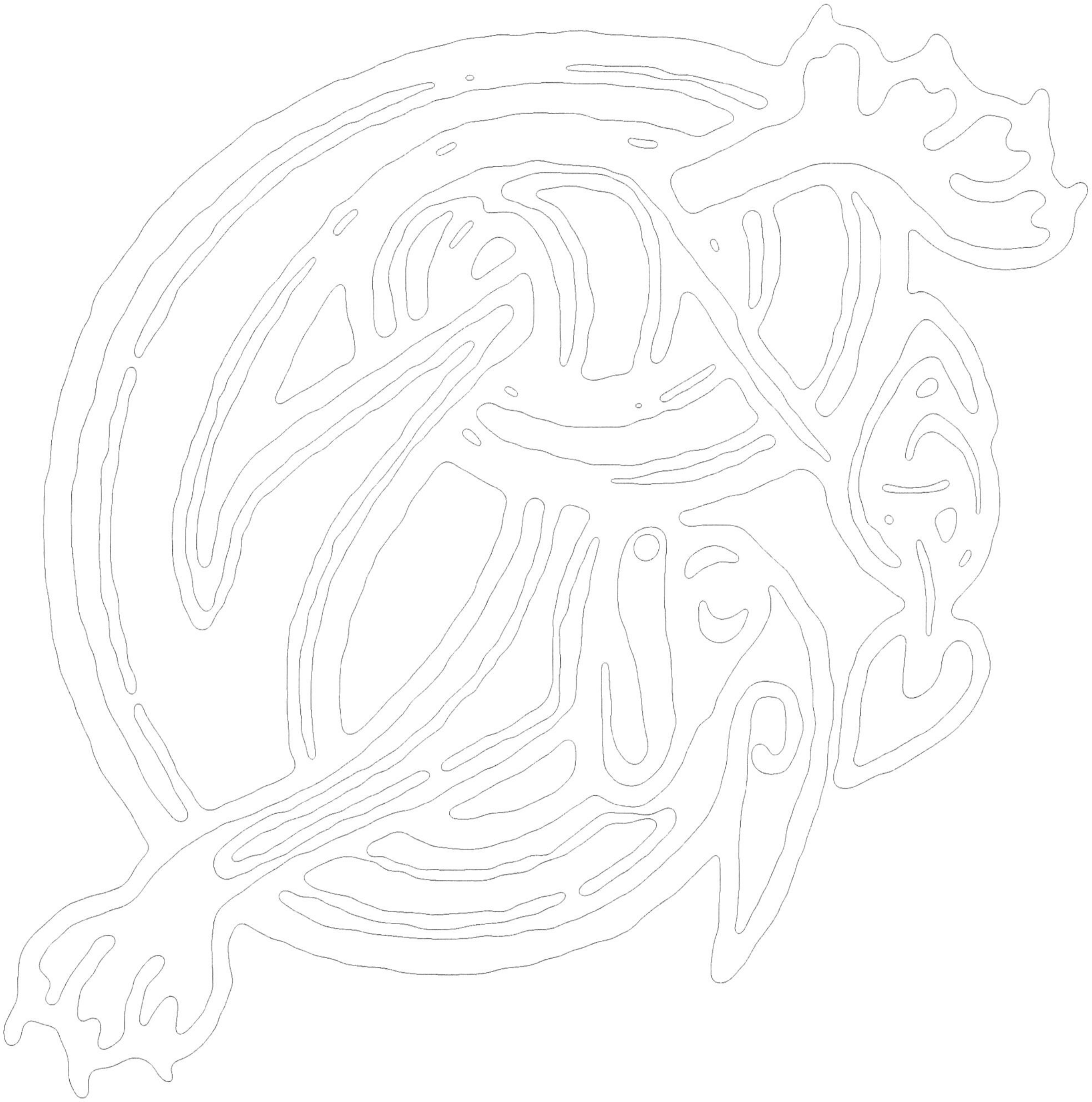

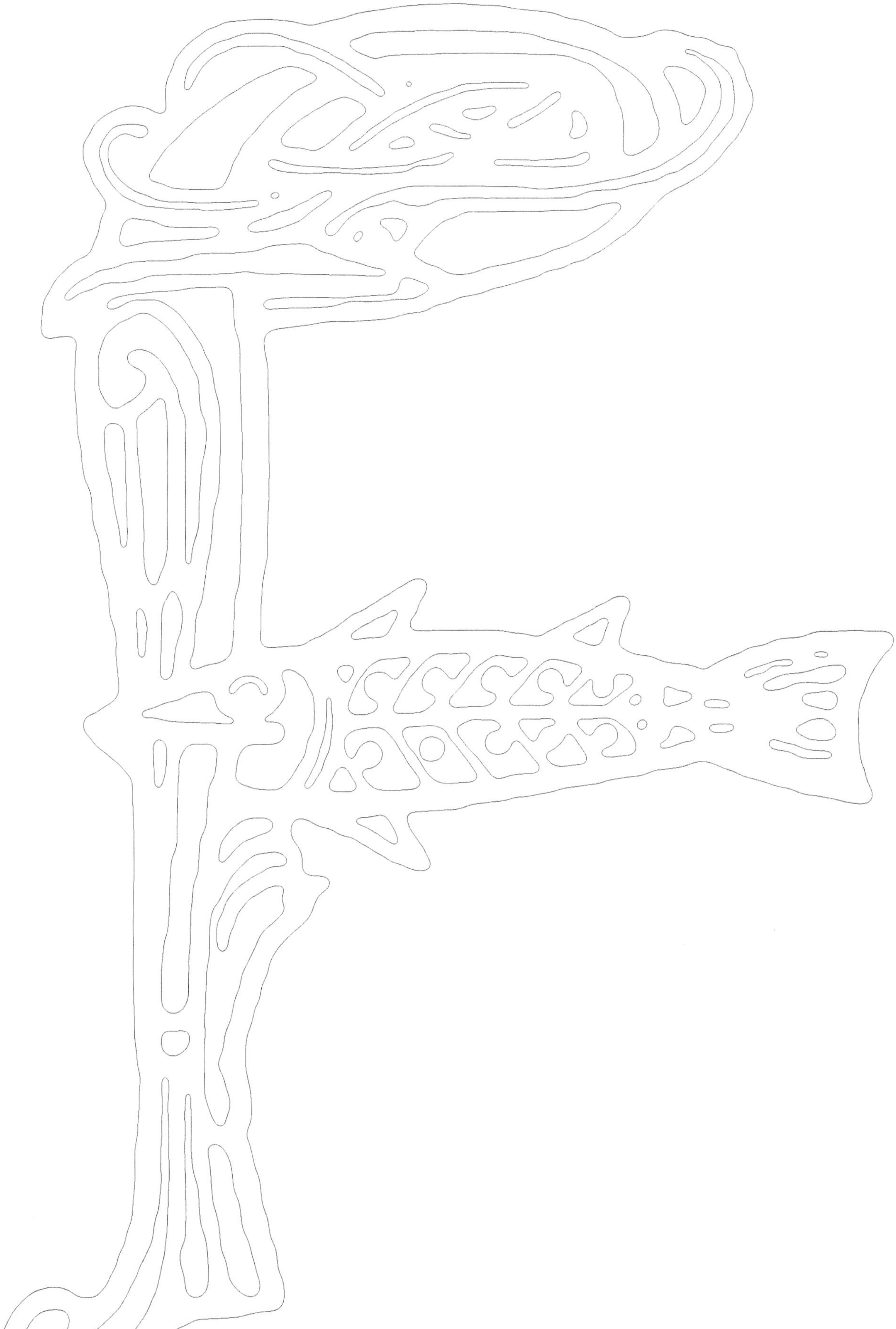

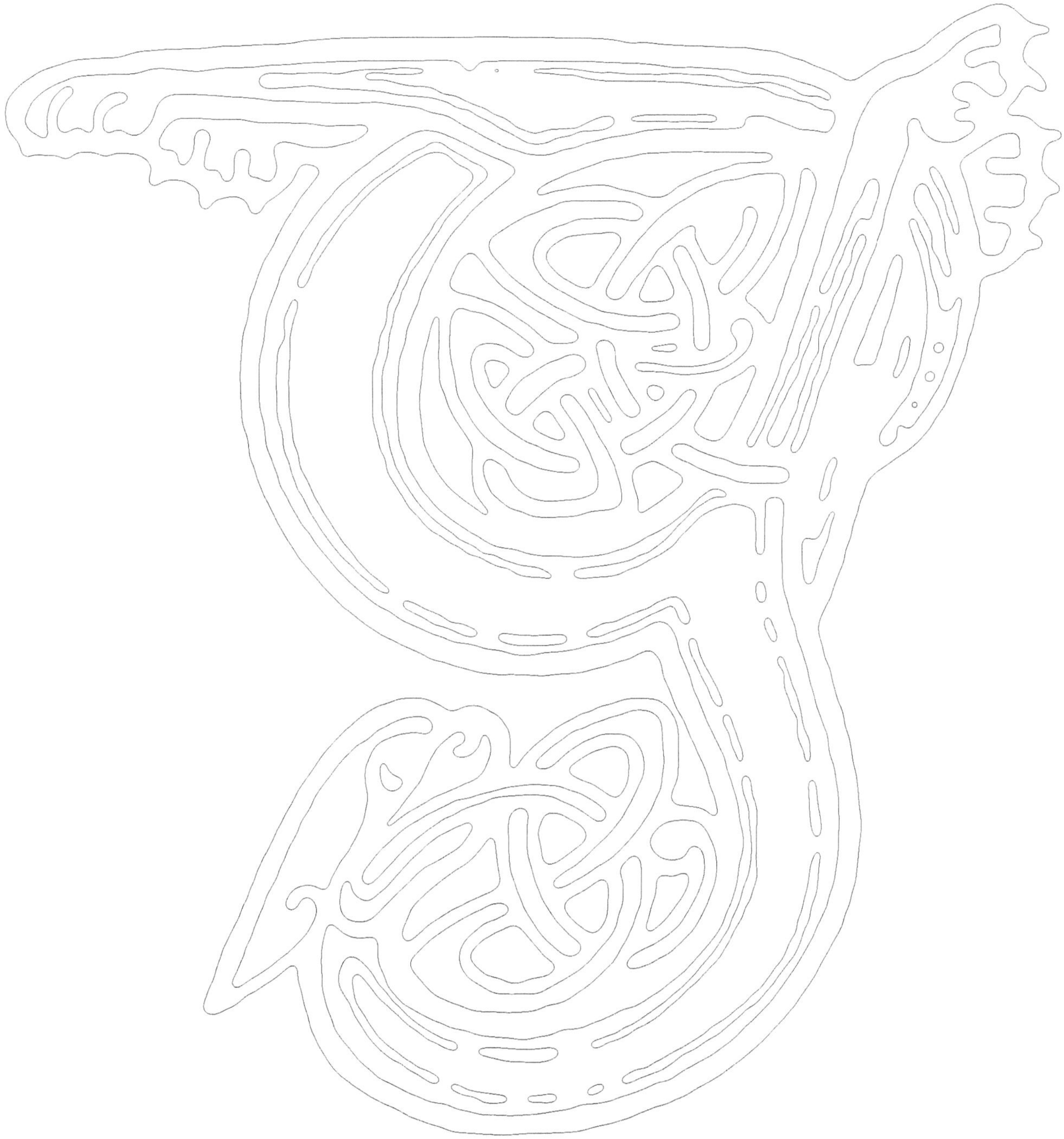

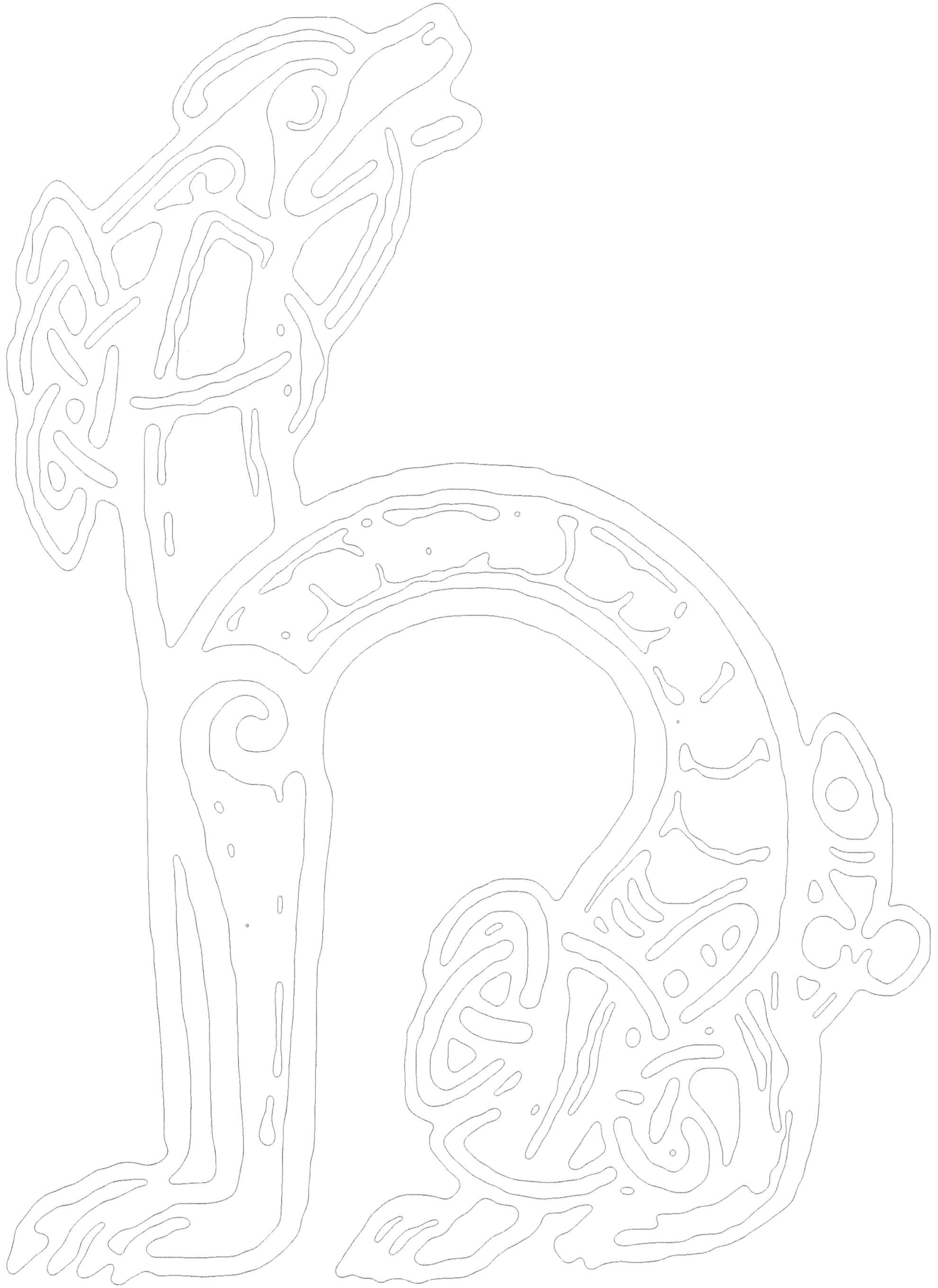

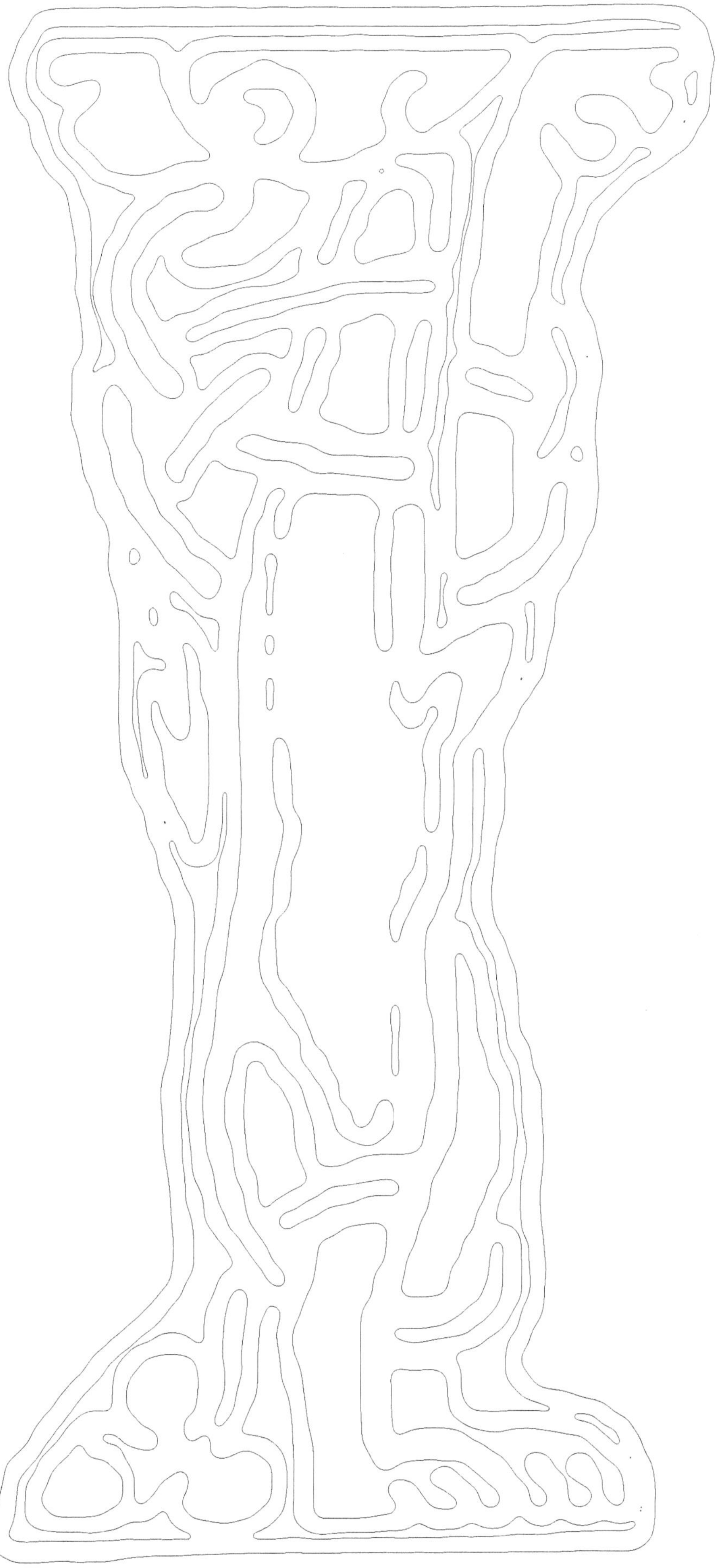

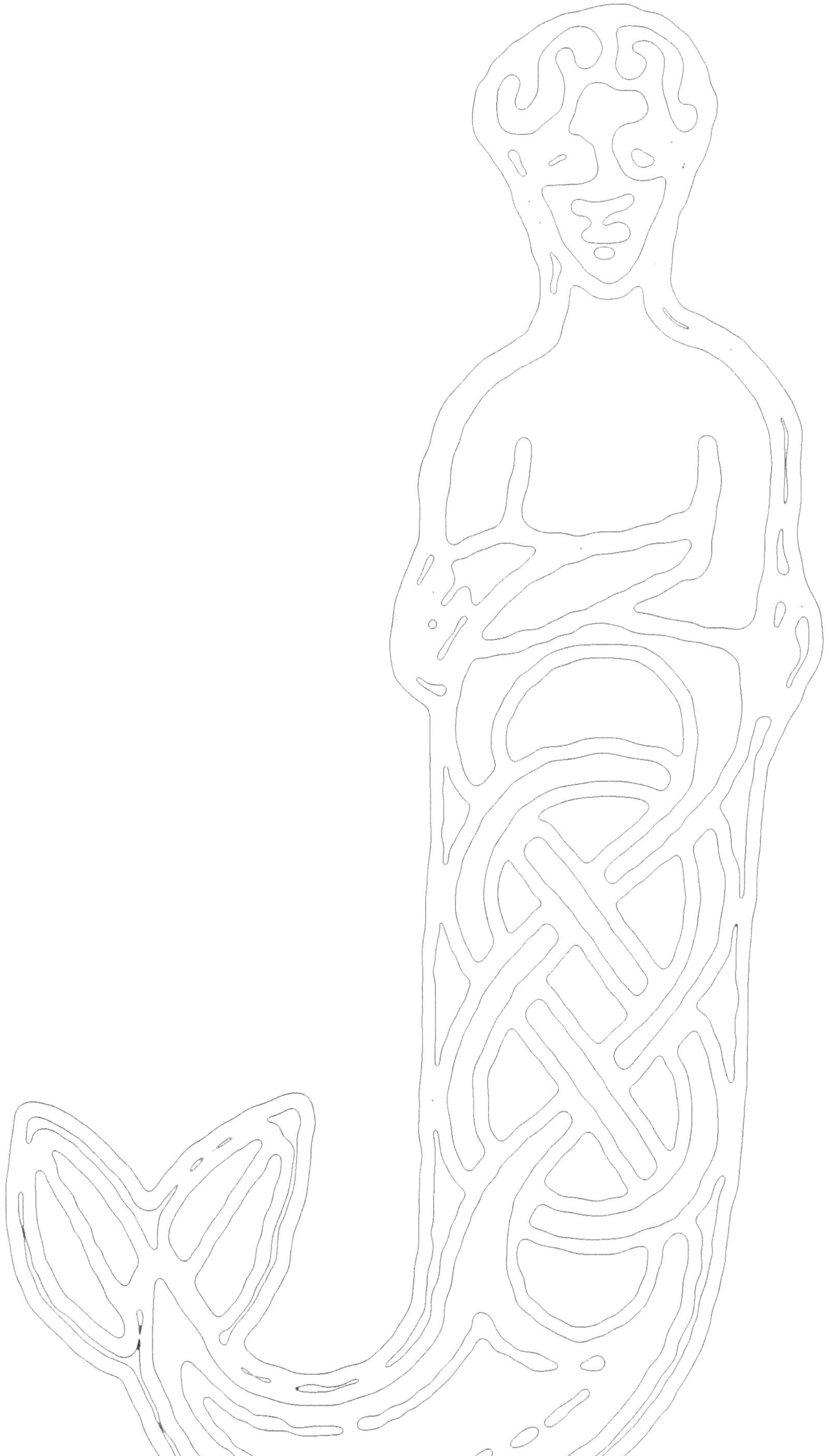

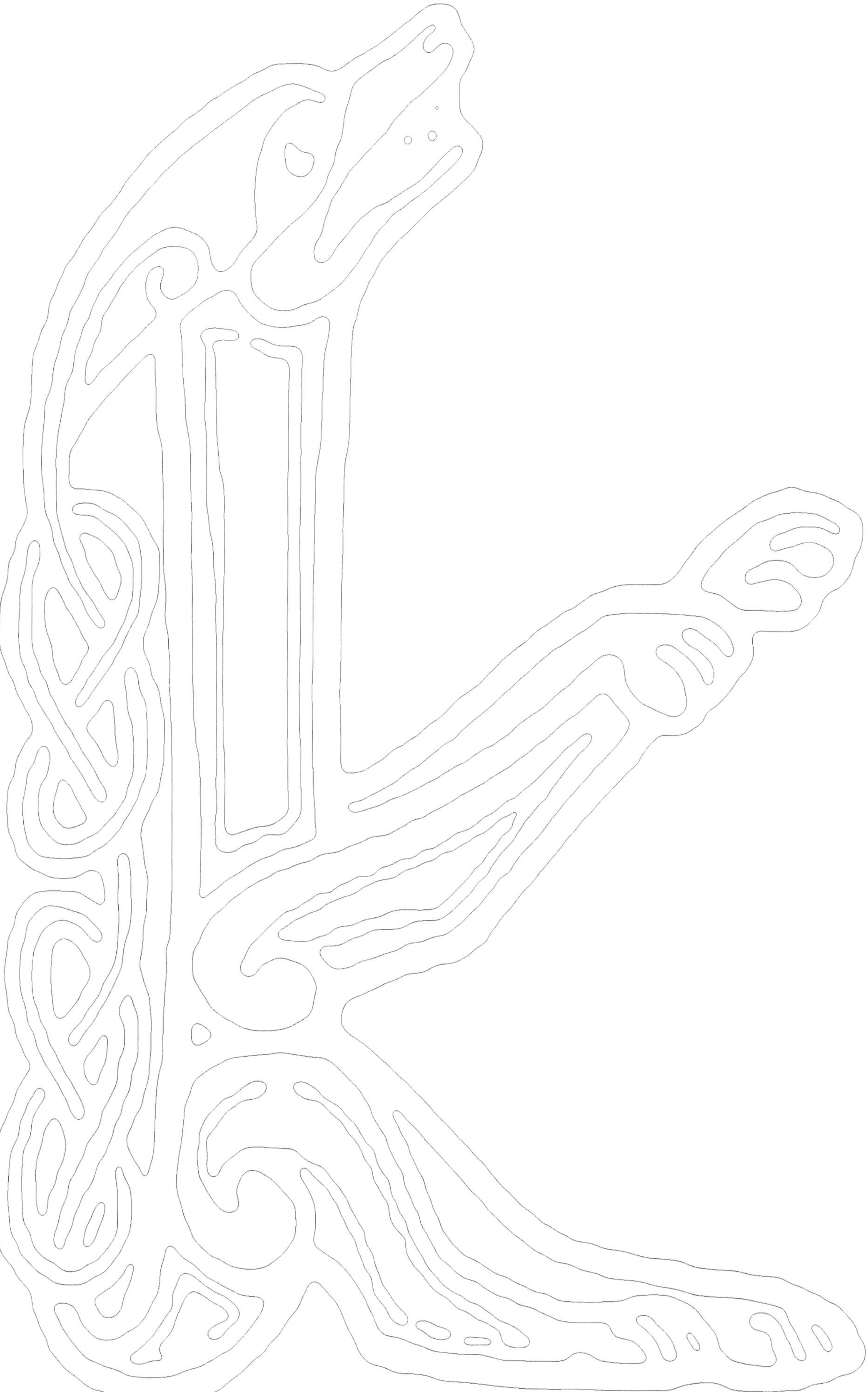

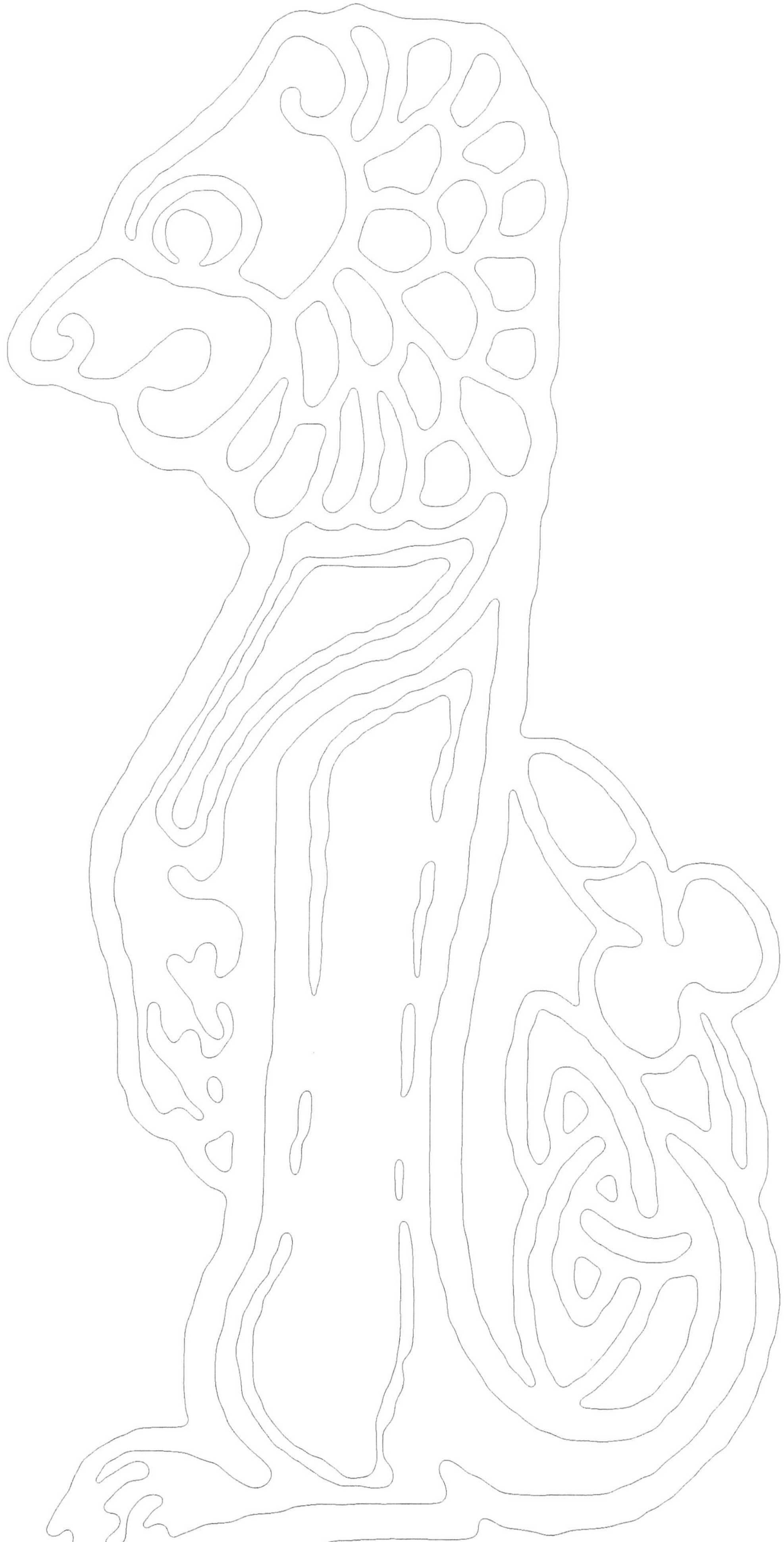

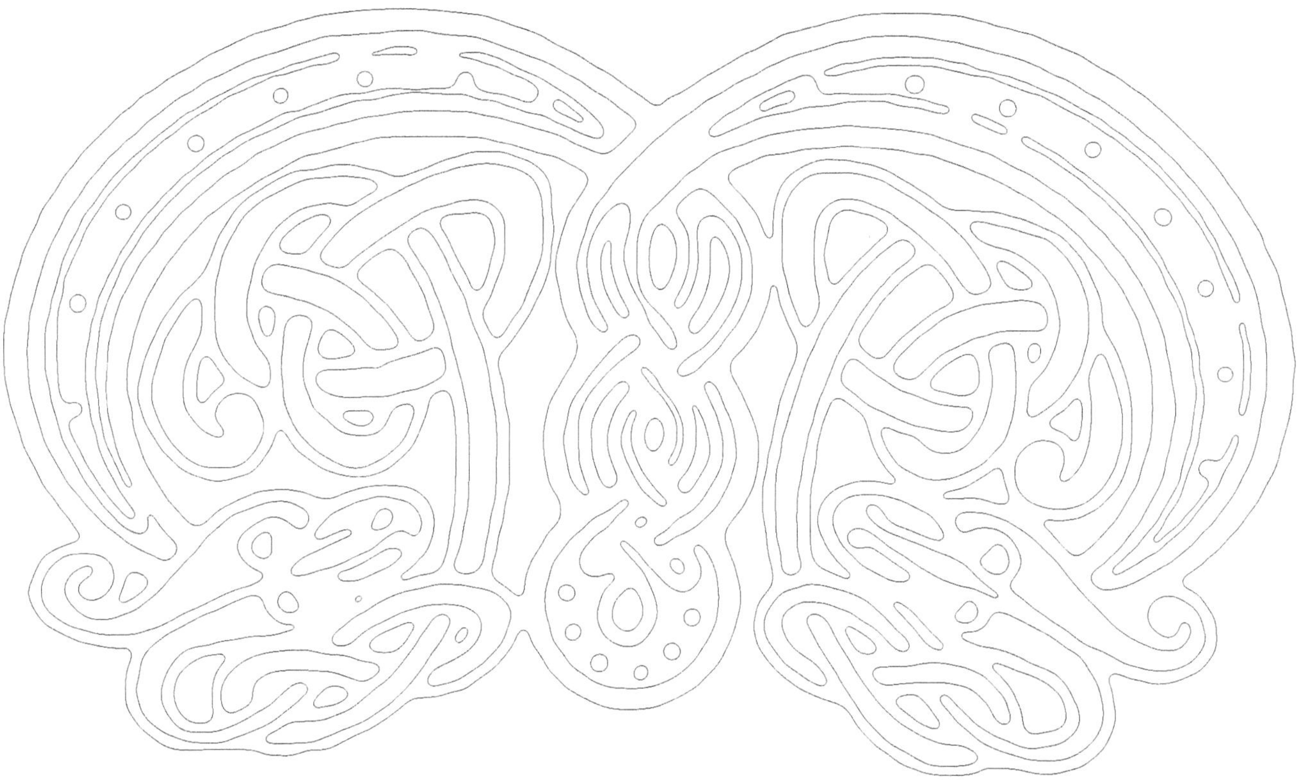

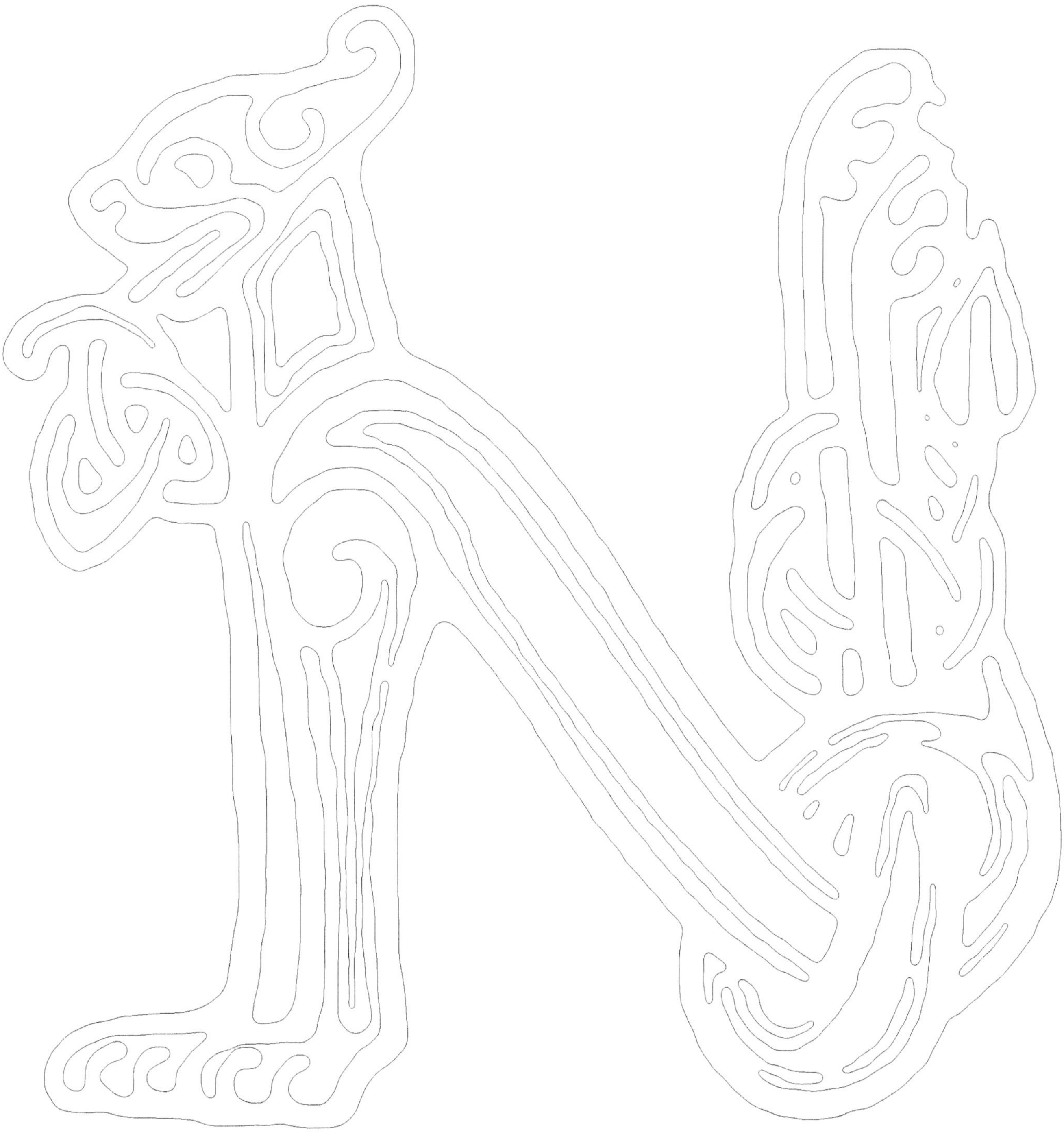

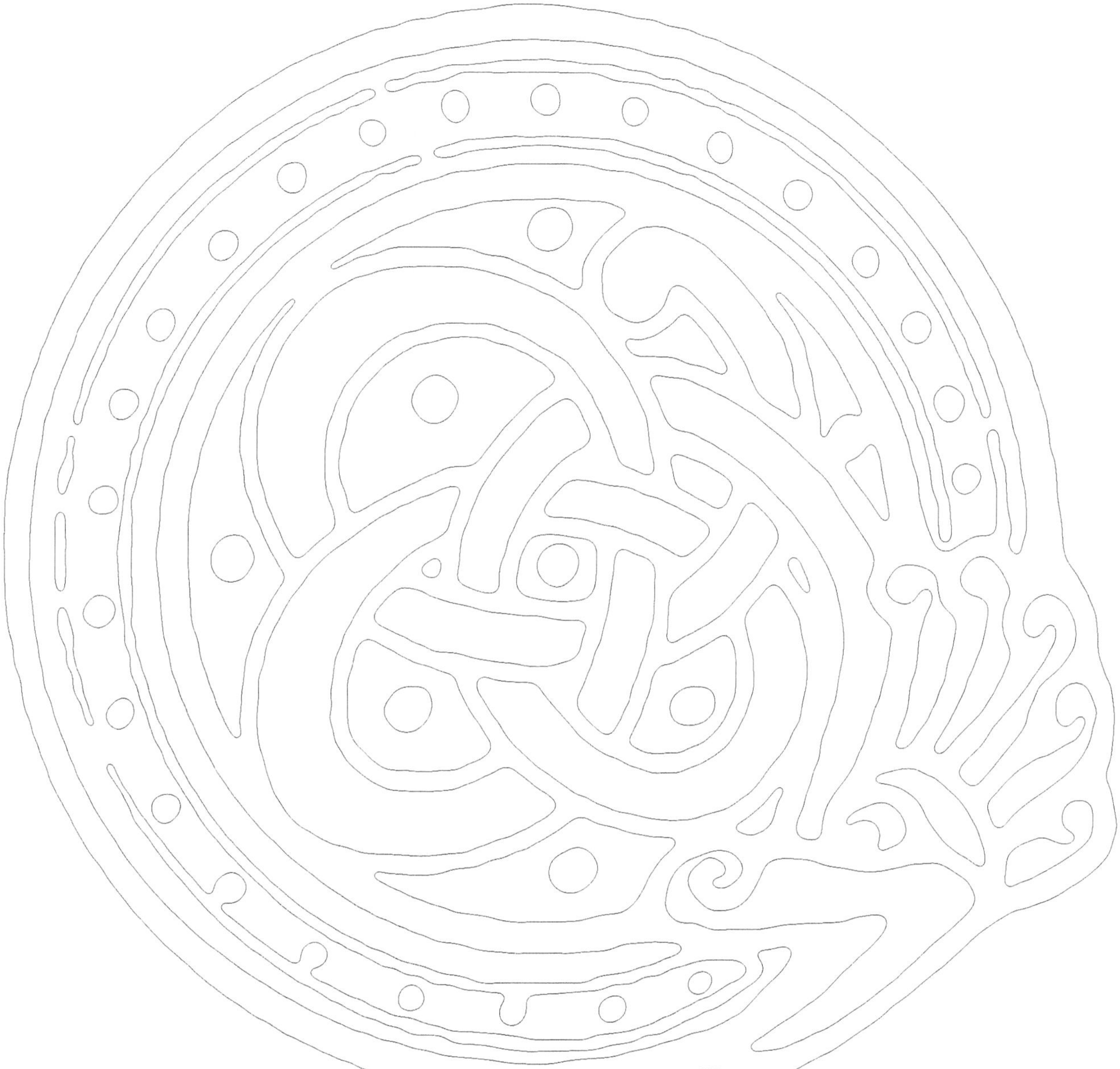

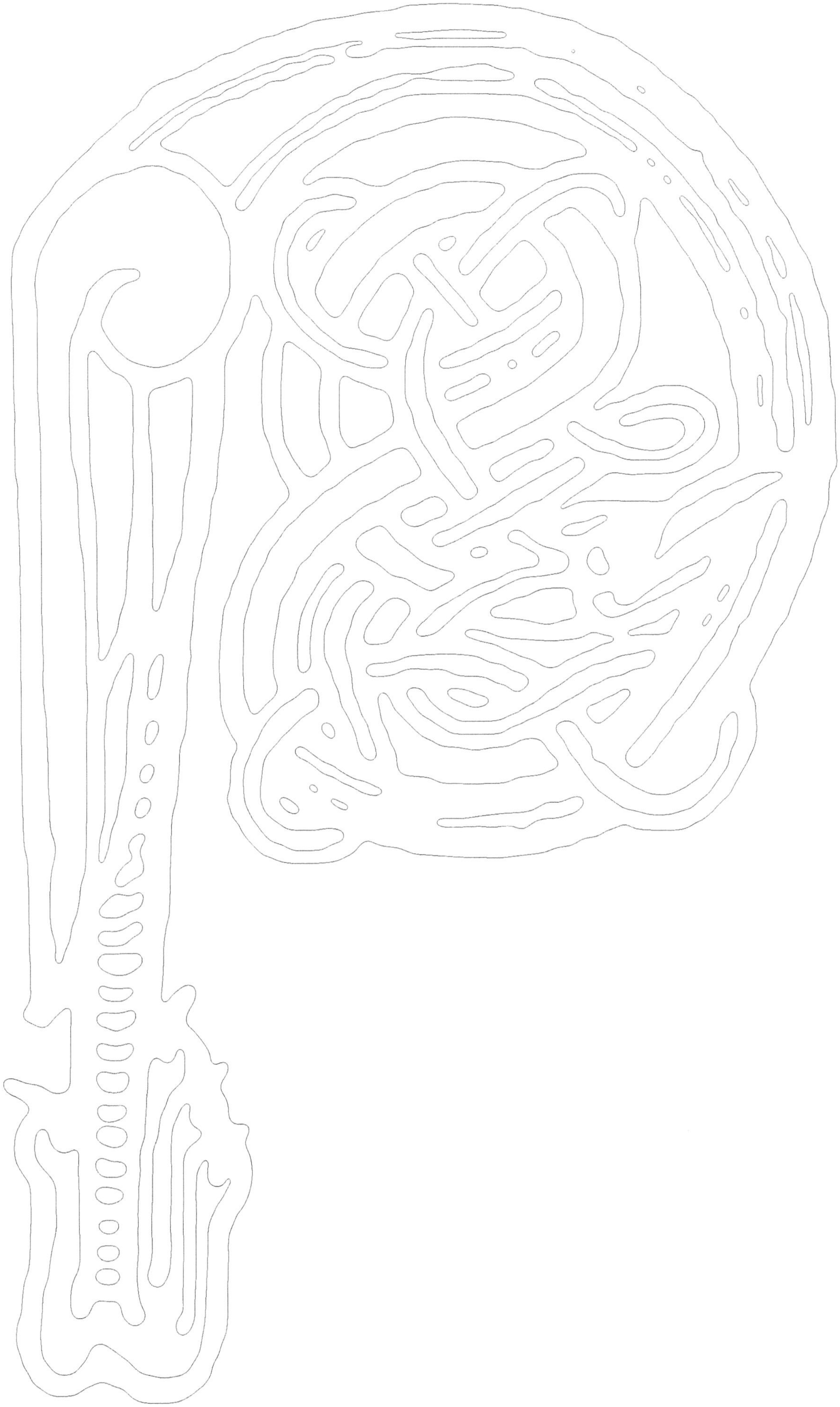

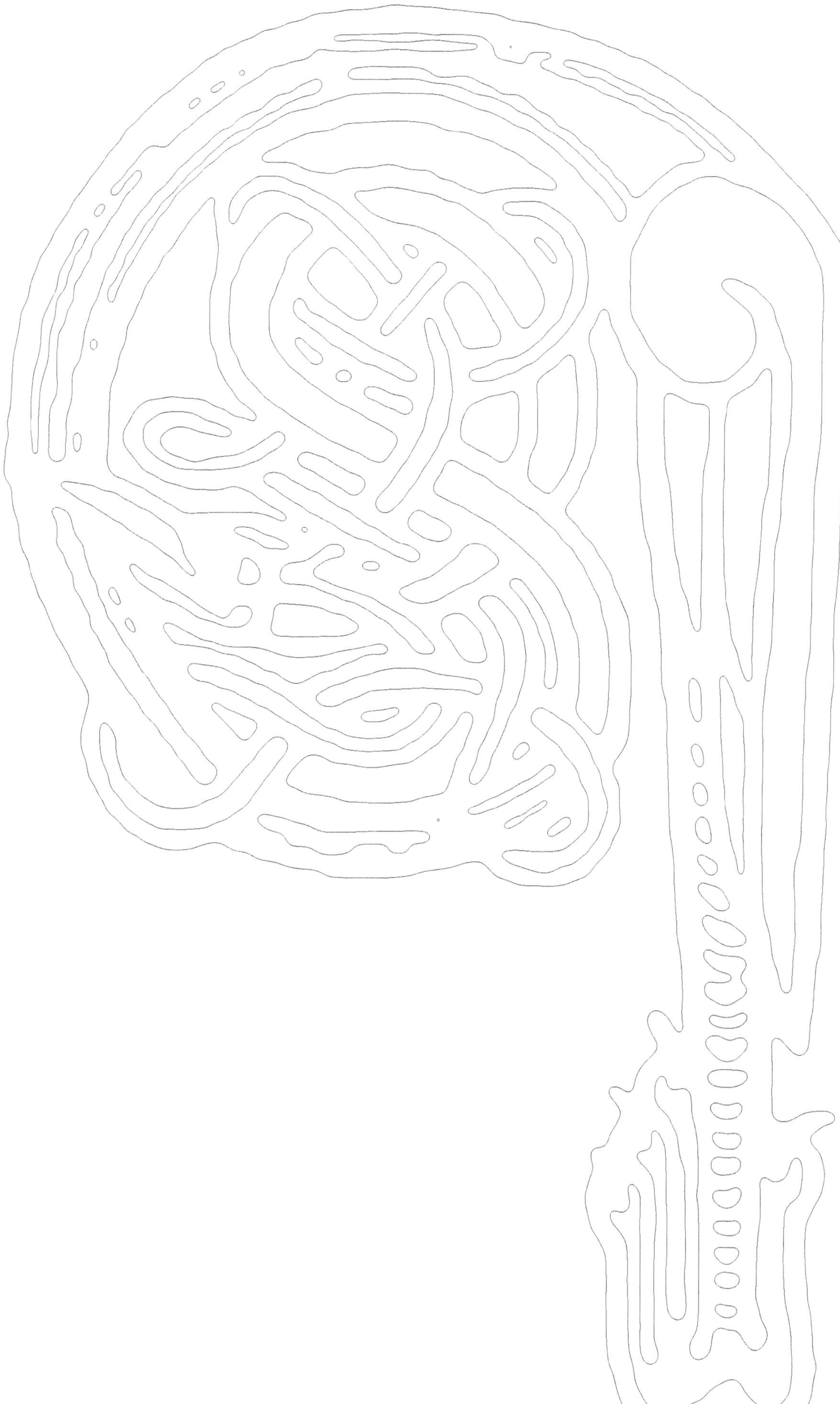

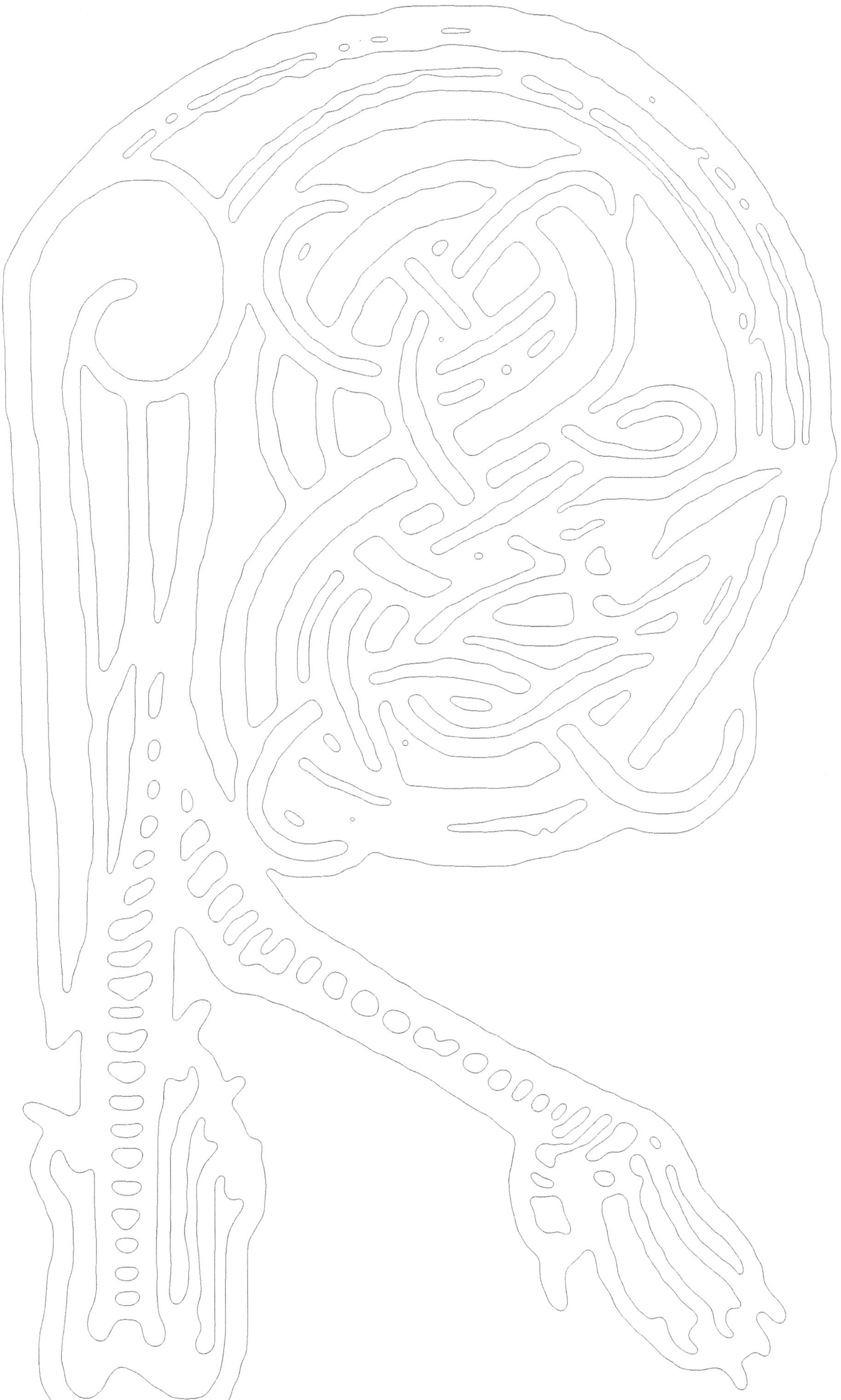

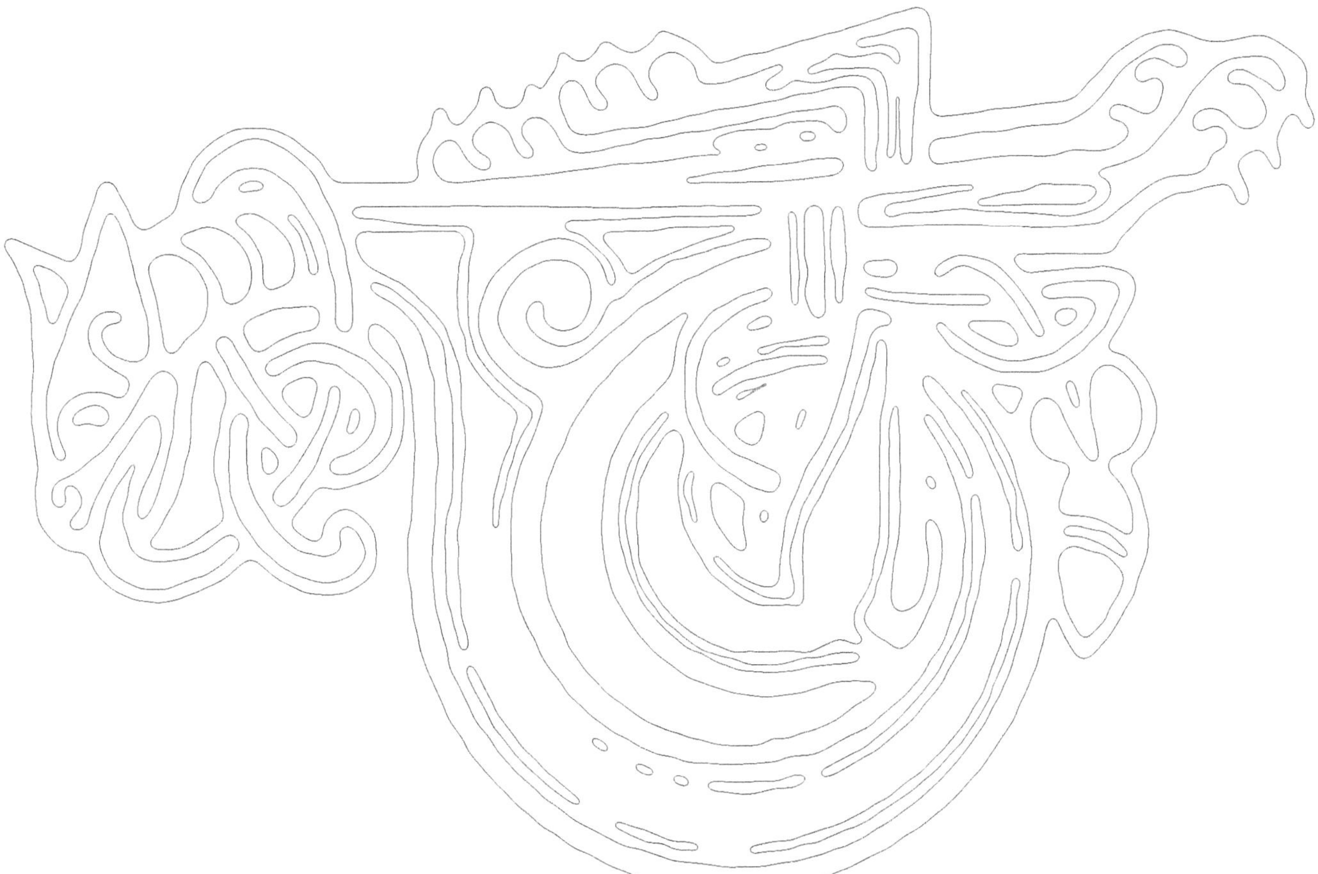

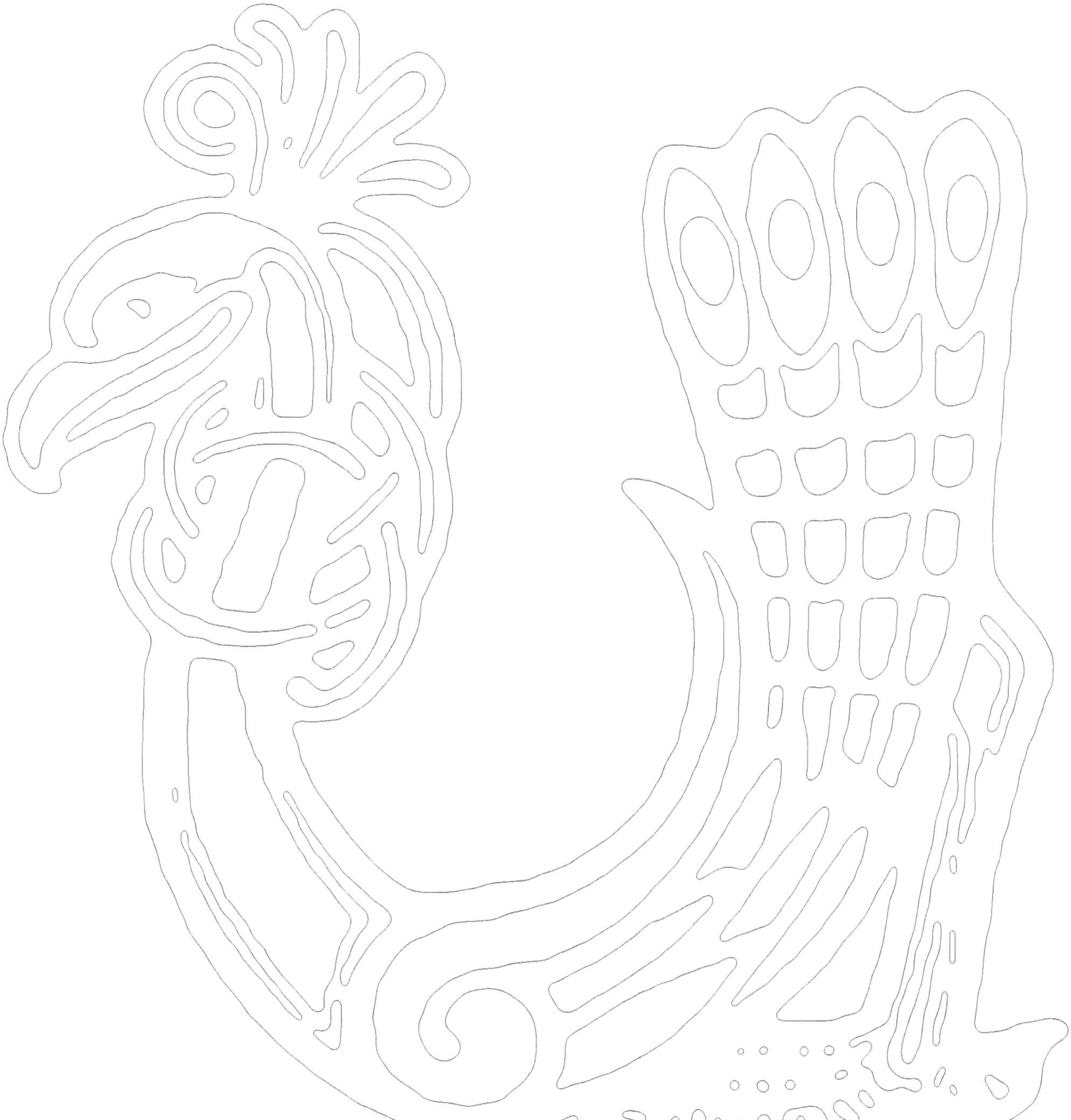

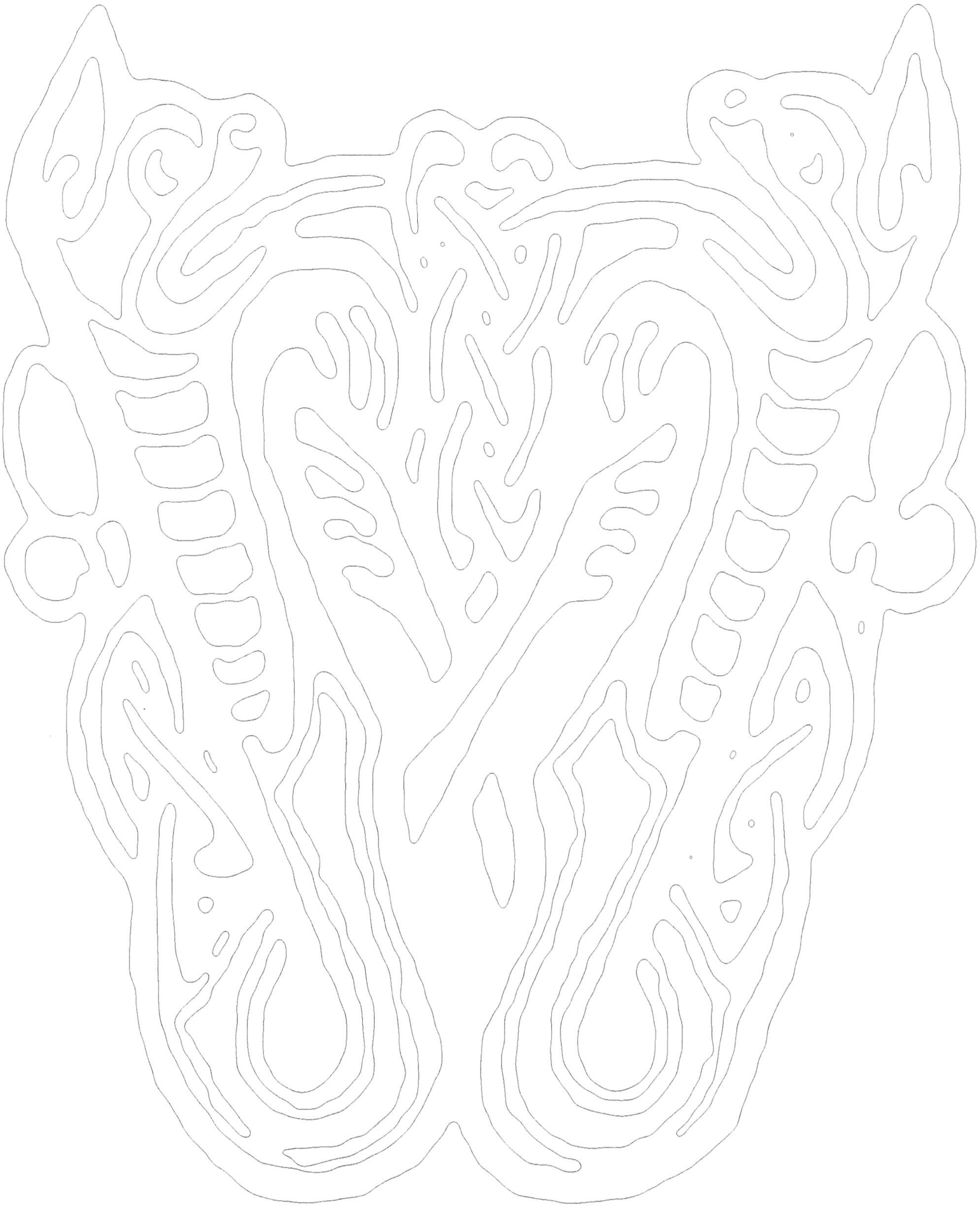

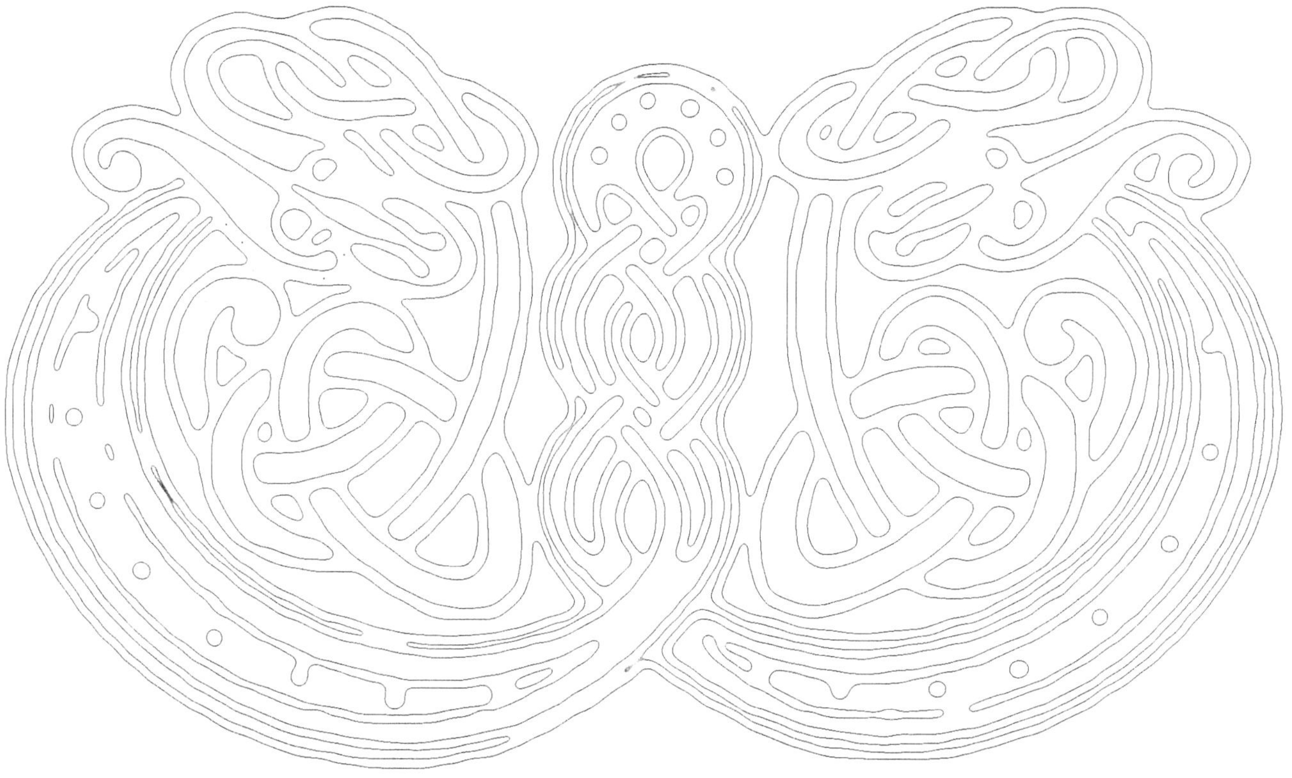

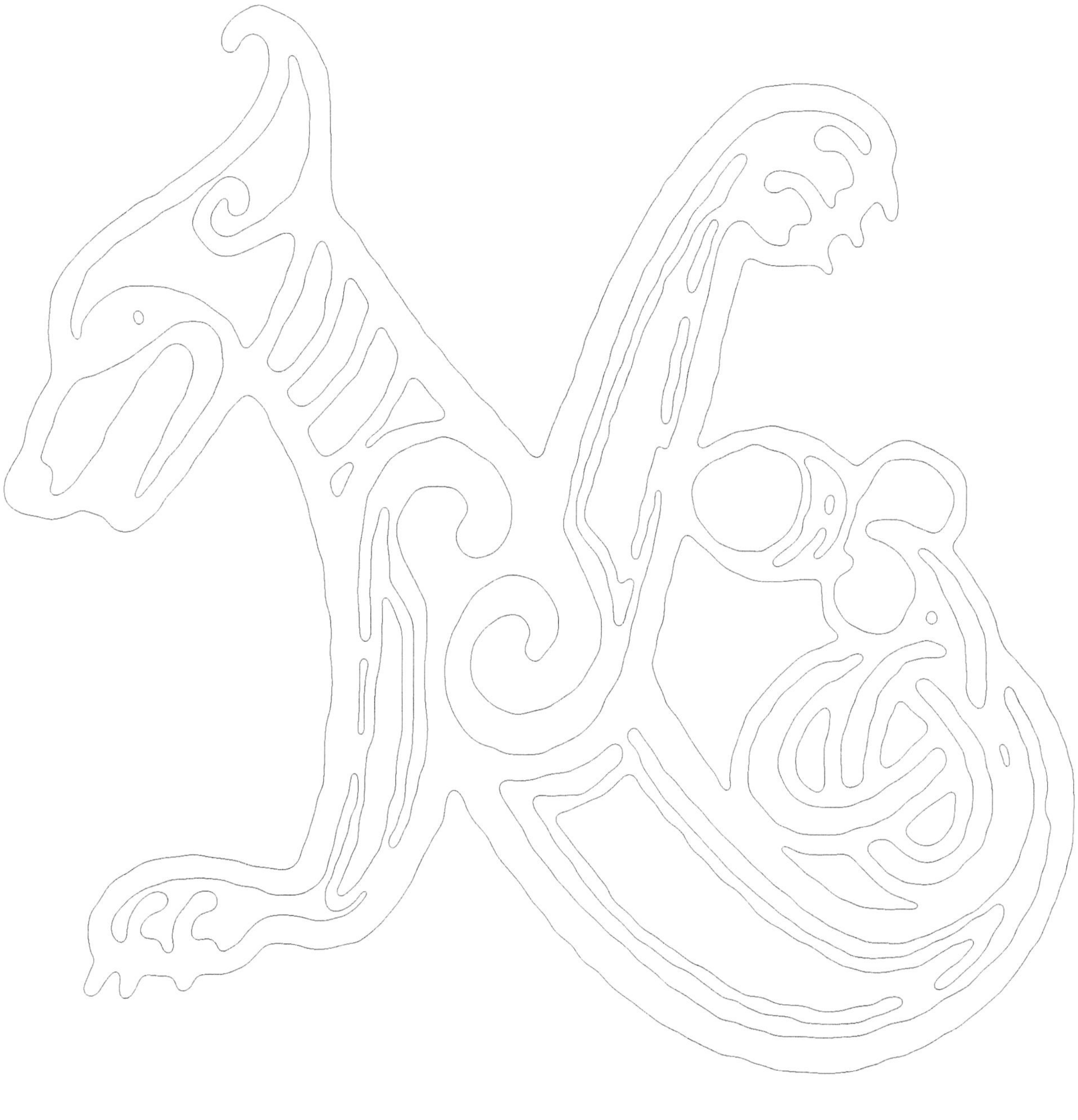

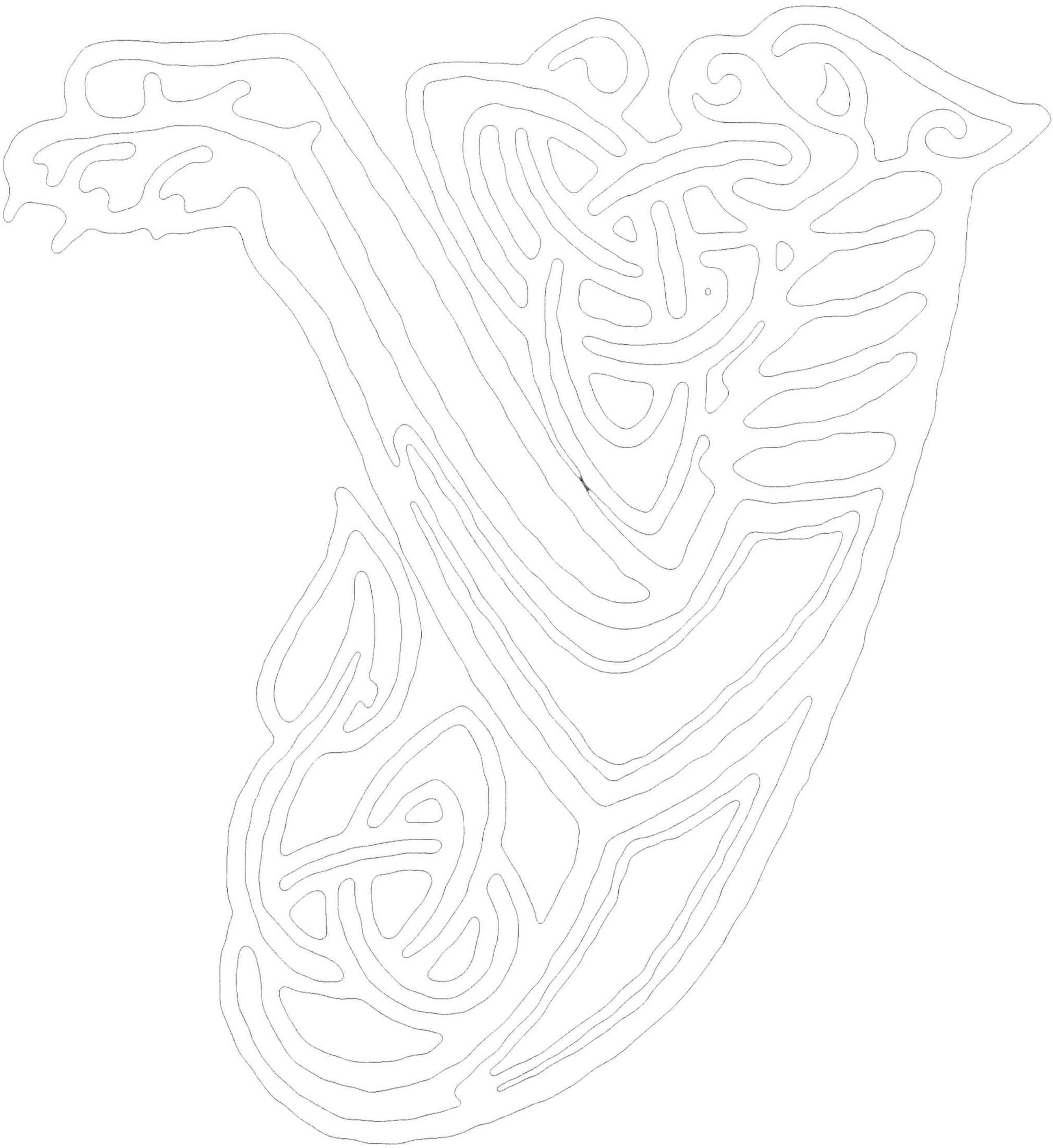

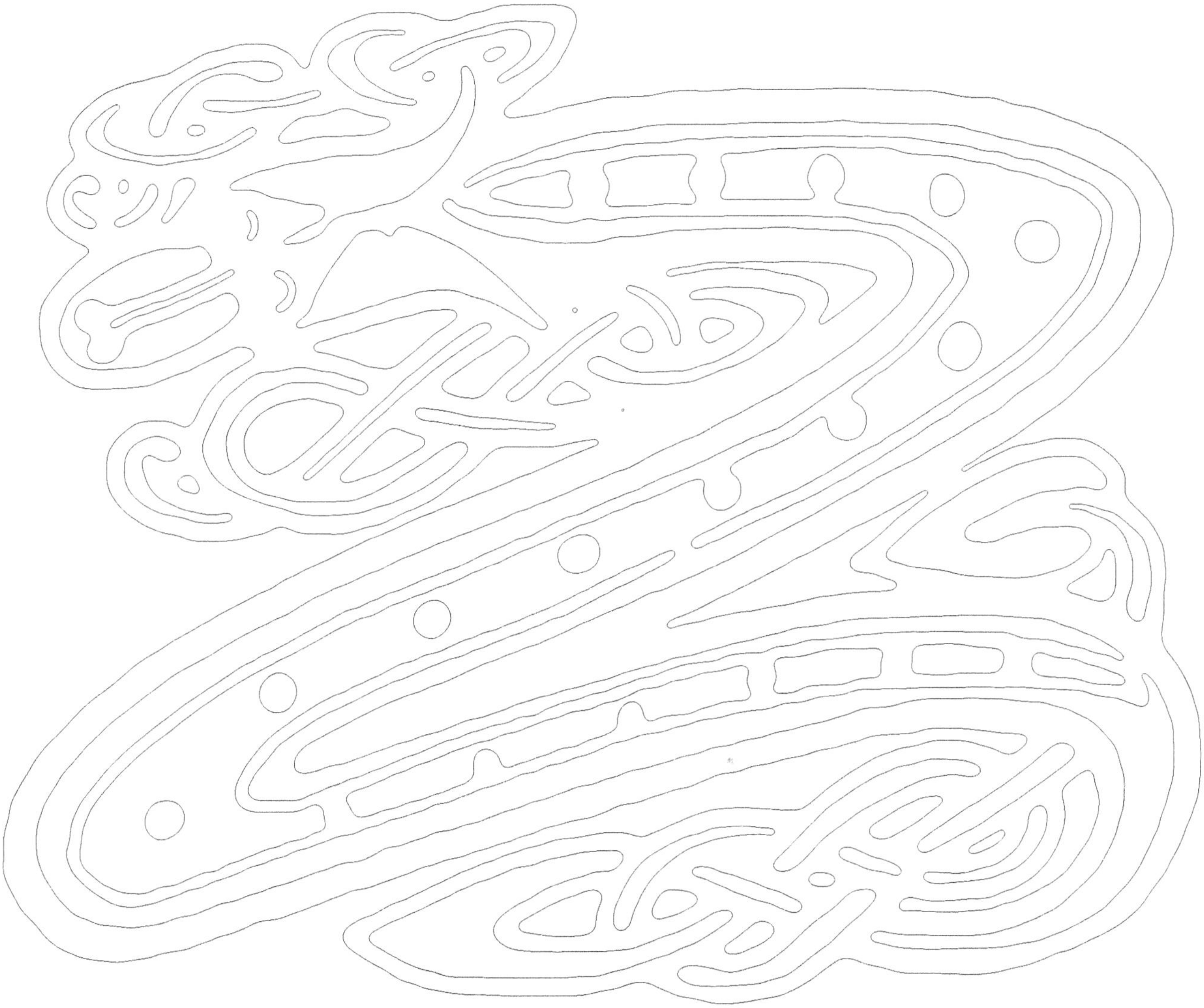

www.ingramcontent.com/pod-product-compliance
Lightning Source LLC
Chambersburg PA
CBHW081126180526
45170CB00008B/3025
* 9 7 8 1 5 4 6 7 1 1 5 8 2 *